DONALD COGGAN

The Name above all Names

LONDON
SPCK

First published 1981
SPCK, Holy Trinity Church, Marylebone Road, London NW1 4DU

Thanks are due to Routledge & Kegan Paul Ltd for permission to reproduce part of Harriet Eleanor Hamilton King's poem *The Disciples*.

The Blackburn Diocese Lent Book 1981

Printed in Great Britain by Hart-Talbot Printers Ltd
Saffron Walden, Essex

ISBN 0 281 03803 1

FOREWORD

I am most grateful to Bishop Donald Coggan for writing this Lent Book for the Diocese of Blackburn. These daily readings and meditations are clearly designed to encourage us to fix our eyes on Jesus. What does he mean to me? There is no more important question in life. During these days in Lent, Bishop Coggan helps us to see what other people found in Jesus for themselves, and to find it for ourselves.

May God use this book to help us to know Jesus better, as saviour of our past, companion of our present, and guide of our future.

✠ **Robert Blackburn**

INVITATION TO EXPLORATION

This small book is an invitation to exploration.

The New Testament is a portrait gallery. All sorts of people have their pictures hung in it–fishermen, tax-gatherers, rulers, saints, prostitutes, scholars, prisoners, refugees, warriors, traitors, martyrs. That is enough to make it a very interesting gallery. But one portrait stands out from the rest in such a way as to make a nonsense of the gallery without it. The portrait is that of Jesus Christ, the one to whom alone can rightly be ascribed the title '*the Lord*'.

The New Testament from one point of view is a collection of the reactions of a wide variety of people to this person. I hold a diamond in my hand. One observer says: 'It's flashing green'. Another: 'It's brilliant red'. Yet a third: 'I see blue'. So it was when Jesus broke into our society. One person saw him one way; to another he appeared very different. In one he aroused hostility; in another, adoration.

On all the writers of the New Testament books he made a tremendous impression; on them he exercised a transforming influence. We are going to study the titles they gave him, the impressions he made on them. As we do so, we shall find ourselves doing much more than indulging in a study of ancient history. We might even hear him say to us: 'Who do *you* say that I am?'

Invitation to exploration . . .

HOW WE SET ABOUT THE EXPLORATION

We have forty-one days for our work–all the weekdays of Lent, and Easter Day itself as the climax.

Each day will begin with a brief **passage from the New Testament.** A **comment** will follow, designed to expound the particular facet of our Lord which we are considering that day. Occasionally we shall spend more than one day on one facet, but not often, for the pictures in our gallery are many. So our study will be far from exhaustive–it is simply aimed to start the reader on his own course of thinking, praying, acting.

Sometimes cross-references to other parts of the Bible are given. It will be well worth while to turn to these and study them. When you can spare the time to read more than the few verses printed for each day, that will be time well spent. In this booklet, the daily readings are from the New English Bible. You may like to compare them with the version which you normally use.

Last will come a **prayer**, or some sentences for meditation. Sometimes the prayer will be repeated, so that we may get familiar with it and it becomes part of us. For example, the prayer we use on Ash Wednesday will be repeated every Monday in the series. It gets close to the heart of what this Exploration is about.

ASH WEDNESDAY

READING Matthew 1.18–25

This is the story of the birth of the Messiah. Mary his mother was betrothed to
Joseph; before their marriage she found that she was with child by the Holy Spirit.
[19]Being a man of principle, and at the same time wanting to save her from
exposure, Joseph desired to have the marriage contract set aside quietly. [20]He had
resolved on this, when an angel of the Lord appeared to him in a dream. 'Joseph
son of David,' said the angel, 'do not be afraid to take Mary home with you as your
wife. It is by the Holy Spirit that she has conceived this child. [21]She will bear a son;
and you shall give him the name Jesus (Saviour), for he will save his people from
their sins.' [22]All this happened in order to fulfil what the Lord declared through the
prophet: [23]'The virgin will conceive and bear a son, and he shall be called
Emmanuel', a name which means 'God is with us'. [24]Rising from sleep Joseph did
as the angel had directed him; he took Mary home to be his wife, [25]but had no
intercourse with her until her son was born. And he named the child Jesus.

JESUS (1)

We end many of our prayers with the words 'through Jesus Christ our Lord'– and often we don't think about them! Let us take them one by one: Jesus–Christ– Lord, and think about them carefully during the coming days.

Jesus is the Name above all names. When he was born, it was as common a name as Tom, Dick or Harry is today. It had a proud history, however, for Jesus is the Latin form of the Hebrew Joshua, and Joshua was one of the giants of the Israelites' saga.

It was Joshua who led the Israelites across the Jordan into the Promised Land. The opening chapters of the book of Joshua tell the exciting story of their entry under the dynamic leadership of Joshua–his name is derived from a word which means to deliver, rescue, save. So St Matthew is quick to point out the significance of the name of the baby whose birth he records in today's reading. The angel said to Joseph: 'You shall give him the name Jesus (Saviour), for he will *save* his people from their sins'. It is Matthew's way of saying: 'A greater than Joshua is here. Joshua saved the Old Israel from tribal enemies; Jesus will save his people from man's greatest and universal enemy, sin'.

Lent provides us with an admirable opportunity to see how this prediction was realized. These studies are designed to help us achieve that end.

To thy Name, Lord Jesus, help me to
  bow the knee and all its worshipping;
  bow the head and all its thinking;
  bow the will and all its choosing;
  bow the heart and all its loving,
today, tomorrow, and all the days of my life.

THURSDAY

READING Acts. 3.1–8, 16

One day at three in the afternoon, the hour of prayer, Peter and John were on their
way up to the temple. [2]Now a man who had been a cripple from birth used to be
carried there and laid every day by the gate of the temple called 'Beautiful Gate', to
beg from people as they went in. [3]When he saw Peter and John on their way into the
temple he asked for charity. [4]But Peter fixed his eyes on him, as John did also, and
said, 'Look at us.' [5]Expecting a gift from them, the man was all attention. [6]And
Peter said, 'I have no silver or gold; but what I have I give you: in the name of Jesus
Christ of Nazareth, walk.' [7]Then he grasped him by the right hand and pulled him
up; and at once his feet and ankles grew strong; [8]he sprang up, stood on his feet, and
started to walk. He entered the temple with them, leaping and praising God as he
went.

[16]And the name of Jesus, by awakening faith, has strengthened this man, whom
you see and know, and this faith has made him completely well, as you can all see for
yourselves.

JESUS (2)

We must spend a second day on the exploration of this word 'Jesus'. It is the key word which opens up the meaning of the Bible and of our Christian faith.

Many people think of Christianity as one of many ethical systems which different civilizations have thrown up from time to time. It is nothing of the sort. It is a revelation of God's activity in delivering us men and women from all that inhibits us from the full life which God intends us to live. It is a divine rescue operation.

This rescue operation centres in Jesus–who he is, what he did, what he does. Though he lived many years ago, he is not a dead hero whose memory we celebrate. He lives, and his life is conveyed to us by his Spirit acting through his Church. The rescue operation goes on; and the evidence can be seen in transformed characters and in the lives of people who can say: 'Once I was blind; now I can see'.

The story in our reading today is of a man who could say: 'Once I was lame, now I can walk'. Peter is careful to point out that he himself is not the healer. It is the powerful name (or person) of Jesus who does it. The faith of the cripple went out to the rescuing Jesus–and the miracle happened!

Jesus! Name of wondrous love!
Name all other names above!
Unto which must every knee
Bow in deep humility.

Jesus! Only Name that's given
Unto all men under heaven,
Whereby man to sin enslaved
Bursts his fetters and is saved.

FRIDAY

READING Luke 2.25–32

There was at that time in Jerusalem a man called Simeon. This man was upright and
devout, one who watched and waited for the restoration of Israel, and the Holy
Spirit was upon him. [26]It had been disclosed to him by the Holy Spirit that he would
not see death until he had seen the Lord's Messiah. [27]Guided by the Spirit he came
into the temple; and when the parents brought in the child Jesus to do for him what
was customary under the Law, [28]he took him in his arms, praised God, and said:

[29]'This day, Master, thou givest thy servant his discharge in peace;
now thy promise is fulfilled.
[30]For I have seen with my own eyes
the deliverance [31]which thou hast made ready in full view of all the nations:
[32]a light that will be a revelation to the heathen,
and glory to thy people Israel.'

CHRIST (1)

The word Christ (Messiah) means one who has been anointed. The Hebrews anointed with oil those who were called to a special office, as, for example, a king or a high priest. (Our own sovereign is anointed at his or her crowning.) So a Hebrew King was called 'the Lord's anointed' (1 Samuel 16.6 AV). It signified a setting apart, a designation by God to a life-work of great significance.

So frequently is this word used of Jesus in the New Testament that it becomes almost a surname, Jesus Christ, Messiah Jesus.

Today and tomorrow we look at two instances when God's revelation dawned on two men–and they discovered that the One for whom their people had been longing was in fact Jesus. *He* was God's Messiah!

The story of old Simeon, 'upright and devout', is a beautiful one. His life was nearly through; he was due for his 'discharge' (v.29). The Holy Spirit was at work in the old man–St Luke mentions the Holy Spirit twice (vv.26, 27). *He* led him to the great discovery that the tiny Babe, brought by his parents to the Temple, was Israel's long-hoped-for Messiah. His circumcision and then his 'presentation to the Lord' (vv.21, 22) was his parents' response to God's designation of Jesus to his unique life-work. He was to effect a deliverance (v.30)–was not his name Jesus (see yesterday's notes)? That deliverance was to be not only for Israel but for 'the heathen', for 'all the nations'. Jesus is the Saviour of the world. He is God's universal answer to man's need.

O Lord, make your ways known upon the earth;
Let all nations acknowledge your saving power.

SATURDAY

READING Mark 8.27–33

Jesus and his disciples set out for the villages of Caesarea Philippi. On the way he
asked his disciples, 'Who do men say I am?' 28They answered, 'Some say John the
Baptist, others Elijah, others one of the prophets.' 29'And you,' he asked, 'who do
you say I am?' Peter replied: 'You are the Messiah.' 30Then he gave them strict
orders not to tell anyone about him; 31and he began to teach them that the Son of
Man had to undergo great sufferings, and to be rejected by the elders, chief priests,
and doctors of the law; to be put to death, and rise again three days afterwards. 32He
spoke about it plainly. At this Peter took him by the arm and began to rebuke him.
33But Jesus turned round, and, looking at his disciples, rebuked Peter. 'Away with
you, Satan,' he said; 'you think as men think, not as God thinks.'

CHRIST (2)

Yesterday we read how old Simeon was given the insight to recognize in the Baby brought to the Temple the long-awaited Messiah. Today we read of another man's insight. It was nothing short of a divine revelation, as St Matthew points out in his record of the story (16. 17).

What a strange mixture of a man Peter was! At one moment he sees in a flash truth hidden from all his colleagues. His spiritual eyesight is clear, and he bursts out: 'You are the Messiah'. The next moment he is the victim of a terrible obtuseness. He seems to be an agent of Satanic temptation to Jesus, not thinking as God thinks but as men do (v.33).

Jesus was aware that Peter's recognition of him as the Messiah might be wrongly interpreted. People might think of the Messiah in terms of power, of the wielding of force in banishing the Roman foe from Jewish soil. At once he begins to make crystal clear that *for him* Messiahship necessarily involves suffering and death (v.31). It is this revelation, this interpretation of Messiahship, which offends Peter and leads to his rebuke of Jesus. How tempting it must have been to Jesus to turn from the prospect of suffering and to think in terms of power? But it could not be. The only way was the way of the Cross.

You Christ are the king of glory,
the eternal Son of the Father.
When you became man to set us free,
You did not abhor the Virgin's womb.
You overcame the sting of death,
and opened the kingdom of heaven to all believers.

LENT 1 Monday

READING Philippians 2.5–11

Let your bearing towards one another arise out of your life in Christ Jesus. 6For
the divine nature was his from the first; yet he did not think to snatch at equality
with God, 7but made himself nothing, assuming the nature of a slave. Bearing the
human likeness, 8revealed in human shape, he humbled himself, and in obedience
accepted even death–death on a cross. 9Therefore God raised him to the heights
and bestowed on him the name above all names, 10that at the name of Jesus every
knee should bow–in heaven, on earth, and in the depths–11and every tongue
confess, 'Jesus Christ is Lord', to the glory of God the Father.

THE LORD

Jesus–Christ–our *Lord*. It is generally recognized that in vv. 6–11 we have a very early Christian hymn, and that in v.11 we have the original baptismal formula, 'Jesus Christ is Lord', and the heart of the Christian creed. (See, for example, Romans 10.9: 'If on your lips is the confession, "Jesus is Lord", and in your heart the faith that God raised him from the dead, then you will find salvation'.)

Here, as we saw on Saturday, are the authentic marks of the Messiahship of Jesus–not the trappings of power, but the self-emptying, the nature of a slave, the human likeness, the death on a cross. Then come the resurrection and ascension, the giving of the name above all other names–Jesus is named *Lord*.

The word *kyrios* is Greek and has very wide meanings. Often it meant nothing more than our 'sir'. In modern Greece a waiter would use this word in addressing a man in a restaurant. But at the other end of the scale, it is used–very frequently indeed–in the Old Testament of Jehovah, *the* Lord. In this passage in Philippians, St Paul clearly has in mind Isaiah 45.23. God is speaking: 'To me every knee shall bend and by me every tongue shall swear'. Now Jesus, crucified, risen, ascended, is the One to whom universal acclamation shall be given, to the glory of God the Father. There is no part of creation–in heaven, on earth, and in the depths (v.10)–over which his domination is not supreme.

This is the divine fiat. We await its full realization.

To thy Name, Lord Jesus, help me to
bow the knee and all its worshipping;
bow the head and all its thinking;
bow the will and all its choosing
bow the heart and all its loving,
today, tomorrow, and all the days of my life.

LENT 1 Tuesday

READING Matthew 1.18–25

This is the story of the birth of the Messiah. Mary his mother was betrothed to
Joseph; before their marriage she found that she was with child by the Holy Spirit.
19Being a man of principle, and at the same time wanting to save her from
exposure, Joseph desired to have the marriage contract set aside quietly. 20He had
resolved on this, when an angel of the Lord appeared to him in a dream. 'Joseph
son of David,' said the angel, 'do not be afraid to take Mary home with you as your
wife. It is by the Holy Spirit that she has conceived this child. 21She will bear a son;
and you shall give him the name Jesus (Saviour), for he will save his people from
their sins.' 22All this happened in order to fulfil what the Lord declared through the
prophet: 23'The virgin will conceive and bear a son, and he shall be called
Emmanuel', a name which means 'God is with us'. 24Rising from sleep Joseph did
as the angel had directed him; he took Mary home to be his wife, 25but had no
intercourse with her until her son was born. And he named the child Jesus.

EMMANUEL

We read again today the same passage which we read last Wednesday. On that day we examined the first name which the evangelist gives us of the newly born child, *Jesus*. Today we note the second, Emmanuel, which means 'God is with us'.

When Christians try to speak about God–and we little mortals cannot do much more than stutter when we try to express in words what we mean by 'God'–we find we must say at least two things. *First*, we must insist on his 'otherness', his holiness, his transcendence. If this created world were to cease, God its Creator, free as he is from the limitations of a created being, would continue to be. *Secondly,* we must insist on his presence throughout the universe. He is not only 'out there'. He is 'here', existing, operating within the universe, within our own world order, within us.

The Hebrews were conscious of the 'otherness' of God–'I dwell in a high and holy place'. But they were also conscious of his closeness to people humble enough to be penitent–'*with him* who is broken and humble in spirit' (Isaiah 57.15). But when Jesus entered the world, 'with him' took on a new meaning. 'God is with us' in a new way, in a human person who, as St Paul put it, 'bears the human likeness' and has been 'revealed in human shape' (Philippians 2.8). Here is the newness of incarnation–'God with us', the 'Word made flesh'. Here is cause for wonder and for worship.

O come, let us adore him,
Christ, the Lord,
Jesus, the Saviour,
Emmanuel, God with us.

LENT 1 Wednesday

READING Matthew 9.35–10.1

So Jesus went round all the towns and villages teaching in their synagogues,
announcing the good news of the Kingdom, and curing every kind of ailment and
disease. [36]The sight of the people moved him to pity: they were like sheep without a
shepherd, harassed and helpless; [37]and he said to his disciples, 'The crop is heavy,
but labourers are scarce; [38]you must therefore beg the owner to send labourers to
harvest his crop.'

[1]Then he called his twelve disciples to him and gave them authority to cast out
unclean spirits and to cure every kind of ailment and disease.

TEACHER (1)

Jesus–Christ–Lord–Emmanuel. What did it mean to have 'God with us', God among us in human flesh? How did it work out? The Gospels give us aspects of Jesus's life and work which help to answer these questions. In the coming days we shall look at some of these aspects in the first three Gospels, leaving those in St John till later.

St Matthew outlines three aspects of Christ's work–teaching, preaching ('announcing the good news of the Kingdom') and healing. We take them in turn.

If you look up the word 'teach' in a concordance of the Bible, you will be surprised to notice how frequently it is used when Christ's ministry is being described. He seems to have taken man's ignorance of the things of God not just as a matter for regret but as an opportunity for his ministry. Here was a task to be tackled, a gap to be filled, a darkness to be illuminated.

When Jesus saw a great crowd, 'his heart went out to them, because they were like sheep without a shepherd; *and he had much to teach them*' (Mark 6.34). It was in large part sheer ignorance that made them what they were, hapless and lost. His role was to be that of a *teacher*. In this way he would shepherd them.

O teach me, Lord, that I may teach
The precious things thou dost impart;
And wing my words that they may reach
The hidden depths of many a heart.

LENT 1 Thursday

READING Matthew 13. 31–35

And this is another parable that he put before them: 'The kingdom of Heaven is like
a mustard-seed, which a man took and sowed in his field. [32]As a seed, mustard is
smaller than any other; but when it has grown it is bigger than any garden-plant; it
becomes a tree, big enough for the birds to come and roost among its branches.'
[33]He told them also this parable: 'The kingdom of Heaven is like yeast, which a
woman took and mixed with half a hundredweight of flour till it was all leavened.'
[34]In all this teaching to the crowds Jesus spoke in parables; in fact he never spoke
to them without a parable. [35]This was to fulfil the prophecy of Isaiah:

'I will open my mouth in parables;
I will utter things kept secret since the world was made.'

TEACHER (2)

Jesus was the supreme master of the art of teaching by parable. To use the imagination as the road to a man's mind and conscience was his favourite method. Sometimes the illustration was brief, as in the two instances in today's reading. Sometimes it was longer, as in the parable of the Prodigal Son (Luke 15.11–32). But always the sayings were so pointed, the illustrations so brightly coloured, that they registered in a man's mind and compelled him to ask: 'What did the Teacher mean by *that*?'

Jesus' skill in using everyday things (seed, soil, weeds, yeast) as illustrations of spiritual truths should be noticed. He avoided the technical language of the theologians and philosophers. So he reached the man in the street. Often he refused to give a straight answer to a straight question, thus compelling the questioner to do some hard thinking for himself. 'What think ye? How does this seem to *you*?' he would say.

Parables had–and have–a way of saying different things to different people. The same story may pierce the darkness of my mind in one way, and the defences of another person's conscience in quite another. That is one of the advantages of the parabolic method of teaching.

It is worth carefully watching Jesus the Teacher at work, pushing back the tide of *ignorance*.

We beseech thee, O God, the God of truth,
that what we know not of things we ought to know,
thou wilt teach us.

LENT 1 Friday

READING Luke 4.16–21

So he came to Nazareth, where he had been brought up, and went to synagogue
on the Sabbath day as he regularly did. He stood up to read the lesson [17]and was
handed the scroll of the prophet Isaiah. He opened the scroll and found the passage
which says,

[18]'The spirit of the Lord is upon me because he has anointed me;
he has sent me to announce good news to the poor,
to proclaim release for prisoners and recovery of sight for the blind;
to let the broken victims go free,
[19]to proclaim the year of the Lord's favour.'

[20]He rolled up the scroll, gave it back to the attendant, and sat down; and all eyes in
the synagogue were fixed on him.
[21]He began to speak: 'Today', he said, 'in your very hearing this text has come
true.'

PREACHER

Preaching and teaching are close cousins. A sermon which does not include some teaching is worth very little. But St Matthew, as we saw on Wednesday, does differentiate between these two activities in the ministry of Jesus.

There is an authoritative note about the word for preaching used by St Matthew (9.35). Strictly it means to do the work of a herald. A herald is a man who is authorized by his sovereign to make the mind of that sovereign known to others. Such was the preaching ministry of Jesus, who came to declare to all who would listen what was in the mind and heart of God. That is the task of all Christian preachers.

What was the message that Christ heralded out? It was, according to Matthew 9.35, 'good news'. Religion, so Jesus made clear, was not an extra burden to be added to already overburdened shoulders. It was not a long list of extra duties to be fulfilled. It was good news of what God was, and of what he had done and was constantly doing.

In our Lord's first sermon, preached in the synagogue of the town in which he had been brought up, he made this very clear. He took as his text the passage from Isaiah 61 in which the 'good news' is spoken of in terms of release for prisoners, recovery of sight for the blind, freedom for broken victims.

The gospel is expressed in a series of indicatives (a 'mood of verbs used to make statements', says the dictionary). Christian imperatives ('a mood . . . used in giving orders') always come second.

In his preaching, Jesus pushed back the tide of *sin*.

We beseech thee, O God, the God of purity,
that where we are sinful thou wilt purge us.

LENT 1 Saturday

READING Luke 8.43–48

Among [the crowds] was a woman who had suffered from haemorrhages for twelve years; and nobody had been able to cure her. [44]She came up from behind and touched the edge of his cloak, and at once her haemorrhage stopped. [45]Jesus said, 'Who was it that touched me?' All disclaimed it, and Peter and his companions said, 'Master, the crowds are hemming you in and pressing upon you?' [46]But Jesus said, 'Someone did touch me, for I felt that power had gone out from me.' [47]Then the woman, seeing that she was detected, came trembling and fell at his feet. Before all the people she explained why she had touched him and how she had been instantly cured. [48]He said to her, 'My daughter, your faith has cured you. Go in peace.'

HEALER

It is clear from a reading of the Gospels that our Lord had a great gift of healing, and that he devoted much of his time and energy to the exercise of this ministry. He took physical and mental sickness very seriously. He recognized that man is an entity of body, mind and spirit, each part of his make-up intimately affecting the other parts. He was concerned that we should be whole. Wholeness and holiness go together in the purpose of God for his children.

In the story we are reading today, our Lord finds himself confronted by a woman who had suffered twelve years from haemorrhages. She feels herself an outcast from society. She exercises her faith in Jesus and touches his garment. We might have dismissed such an act as 'mere superstition'. Jesus does nothing of the sort. 'My daughter', he says, 'your faith has cured you. Go into peace' (v.48). '*Into* peace'–that is the literal translation. She had lived in anxiety, fear, isolation. Now, since her contact with Jesus, she can go into a new life–of wholeness, haleness, health, holiness.

This is but one of a long series of instances recorded in the Gospels of our Lord's exercise of his ministry of healing. The stories are vivid records of the 'release . . . the recovery . . . the freedom' which he had proclaimed as the essence of his life work (see yesterday's reading and notes).

In his healing, Jesus pushed back the tide of *sickness*.

We beseech thee, O God, the God of health,
that where we are sick thou wilt heal us.

LENT 2 Monday

READING Luke 13.10–17

One Sabbath he was teaching in a synagogue, 11and there was a woman there
possessed by a spirit that had crippled her for eighteen years. She was bent
double and quite unable to stand up straight. 12When Jesus saw her he called her
and said, 'You are rid of your trouble.' 13Then he laid his hands on her, and at
once she straightened up and began to praise God. 14But the president of the
synagogue, indignant with Jesus for healing on the Sabbath, intervened and said
to the congregation, 'There are six working-days: come and be cured on one of
them, and not on the Sabbath.' 15The Lord gave him his answer: 'What hypocrites
you are!' he said. 'Is there a single one of you who does not loose his ox or his
donkey from the manger and take it out to water on the Sabbath? 16And here is
this woman, a daughter of Abraham, who has been kept prisoner by Satan for
eighteen long years: was it wrong for her to be freed from her bonds on the
Sabbath?' 17At these words all his opponents were covered with confusion, while
the mass of the people were delighted at all the wonderful things he was doing.

FIGHTER

When we speak of Jesus as a fighter, we are really continuing the train of thought which occupied us last week–Jesus the teacher, fighting ignorance; Jesus the preacher, fighting sin; Jesus the healer, fighting sickness. Emmanuel, God with us!

Today's story of our Lord's meeting with the woman with the twisted back is yet one more example of his refusal to acquiesce in life's tragedies and leave them as they are. As he looks at this woman's distorted body, he does not say 'God wills it' and so dismiss her with a touch of fatalism. Rather, he sees that a sinister force has been at work ('Satan has bound her'), and he goes into action to combat that force.

This is not to affirm that Jesus held that suffering was in all cases the direct result of the sufferer's sin. That would indeed be an over-simplification of a monstrous kind. In fact, he went out of his way to deny this (see Luke 13.1–5). But it is to affirm that Jesus found himself confronted by a vast and sinister force which manifested itself in all kinds of ignorance, sin and sickness; and to be confronted by this was to be affronted by it. He could not remain idle in the face of this force. He threw himself against it in a ministry which eventually cost him his life. He was a fighter to the end.

To thy Name, Lord Jesus, help me to
  bow the knee and all its worshipping;
  bow the head and all its thinking;
  bow the will and all its choosing;
  bow the heart and all its loving,
today, tomorrow, and all the days of my life.

LENT 2 Tuesday

READING Matthew 4.1–10

Jesus was then led away by the Spirit into the wilderness, to be tempted by the devil.
2 For forty days and nights he fasted, and at the end of them he was famished. 3 The
tempter approached him and said, 'If you are the Son of God, tell these stones to
become bread.' 4 Jesus answered, 'Scripture says, "Man cannot live on bread alone;
he lives on every word that God utters." '
5 The devil then took him to the Holy City and set him on the parapet of the
temple. 6 'If you are the Son of God,' he said, 'throw yourself down; for Scripture
says, "He will put his angels in charge of you, and they will support you in their
arms, for fear you should strike your foot against a stone." ' 7 Jesus answered him,
'Scripture says again, "You are not to put the Lord your God to the test." '
8 Once again, the devil took him to a very high mountain, and showed him all the
kingdoms of the world in their glory. 9 'All these', he said, 'I will give you, if you will
only fall down and do me homage.' 10 But Jesus said, 'Begone, Satan! Scripture says,
"You shall do homage to the Lord your God and worship him alone." '

SERVANT (1)

It is clear from a reading of the Gospels that Jesus had pondered deeply on the Old Testament Scriptures (as we now call them) before he began his public ministry. Two books appear to have especially influenced his thinking on the nature of the ministry he was to fulfil, namely Deuteronomy and Isaiah. We shall consider the influence of Deuteronomy today, and that of Isaiah tomorrow.

The three temptations which assailed our Lord after his baptism and before he 'went public' had to do specifically with this matter. Should it be a ministry devoted to alleviating men's physical needs? After all, Jesus cared deeply for people's health (vv. 2–4). Jesus refused this temptation, quoting Deuteronomy 8.3. Then, what about a sensational show (vv.5–7)? Again he refused, quoting Deuteronomy 6.16. Then again, what about a demonstration of sovereign power (vv.8–10)? Yet again he refused, quoting Deuteronomy 6.13. The people longed for food (who could blame them?), for fun (life was drab under Roman rule), for force which would drive the occupying armies into the sea. These desires were natural enough.

But if they were met, men's deepest needs would still remain unmet. Jesus knew this. Hence his threefold 'No' to what he could only regard as a diabolical attempt to make him swerve from the primary purpose of his mission. *That* could only be fulfilled if he took upon him the form of a *servant*.

O God, our salvation and truth, grant that we thy children, rejecting the proud wisdoms of the world, may betake ourselves to the Cross of thy dear Son, to walk by its way, to repose in its shadow, to venerate its mercy and to embrace its scorn; through the same Jesus Christ our Lord.

LENT 2 Wednesday

READING Mark 10.35–45

James and John, the sons of Zebedee, approached him and said, ‘Master, we should
like you to do us a favour.’ 36‘What is it you want me to do?’ he asked. 37They
answered, ‘Grant us the right to sit in state with you, one at your right and the other
at your left.’ 38Jesus said to them, ‘You do not understand what you are asking. Can
you drink the cup that I drink, or be baptized with the baptism I am baptized with?’
39‘We can’, they answered. Jesus said, ‘The cup that I drink you shall drink, and the
baptism I am baptized with shall be your baptism; 40but to sit at my right or left is not
for me to grant; it is for those to whom it has already been assigned.’
41When the other ten heard this, they were indignant with James and John.
42Jesus called them to him and said, ‘You know that in the world the recognized
rulers lord it over their subjects, and their great men make them feel the weight of
authority. 43That is not the way with you; among you, whoever wants to be great
must be your servant, 44and whoever wants to be first must be the willing slave of all.
45For even the Son of Man did not come to be served but to serve, and to give up his
life as a ransom for many.’

SERVANT (2)

If the book of Deuteronomy was influential on the mind of Jesus in determining the nature of the ministry which he was to pursue, the book of Isaiah was probably even more influential. This was especially true of those four passages which are known as the servant songs, namely 42. 1–4; 49. 1–6; 50. 4–11; and 52.13—53.12. In these passages, a figure is depicted who was living in a very close relationship with God, receptive of his word, deeply influenced by his Spirit, tender in his approach to people, entrusted with a message not only to Israel but also to the nations beyond, but undergoing insults and suffering of an appalling kind, stricken on behalf of the people to whom he was sent. Here was a figure, not of power as men reckon power, but of service which led to agony and death.

With this figure, so movingly described by the prophet, Jesus associated himself. When James and John asked for seats reserved for men of great authority, Jesus had to point out to them that, if they were to be his true followers, their discipleship would involve not the trappings of majesty but a cup of suffering and a baptism of tribulation, perhaps leading even to martyrdom–‘for the Son of Man did not come to be served but to serve, and to give up his life as a ransom for many’.

Almighty God, whose most dear Son went not up to joy but first he suffered pain, and entered not into glory before he was crucified; mercifully grant that we, walking in the way of the Cross, may find it none other than the way of life and peace; through the same thy Son Jesus Christ our Lord.

LENT 2 Thursday

READING Matthew 8.19–20; 13.36–43

A doctor of the law came up, and said, 'Master, I will follow you wherever you
go.' [20]Jesus replied, 'Foxes have their holes, the birds their roosts; but the Son of
Man has nowhere to lay his head.'

[36]He then dismissed the people, and went into the house, where his disciples came
to him and said, 'Explain to us the parable of the darnel in the field.' [37]And this
was his answer: 'The sower of the good seed is the Son of Man. [38]The field is the
world; the good seed stands for the children of the Kingdom, the darnel for the
children of the evil one. [39]The enemy who sowed the darnel is the devil. The
harvest is the end of time. The reapers are angels. [40]As the darnel, then, is
gathered up and burnt, so at the end of time [41]the Son of Man will send out his
angels, who will gather out of his kingdom whatever makes men stumble, and all
whose deeds are evil, [42]and these will be thrown into the blazing furnace, the place
of wailing and grinding of teeth. [43]And then the righteous will shine as brightly as
the sun in the kingdom of their Father. If you have ears, then hear.'

SON OF MAN

There is something mysterious about this phrase which occurs so often in the first three Gospels. It has about it a reminder of a passage in Daniel 7.13 where it represents, in the symbolism of the vision, 'the people of the saints of the Most High'. But in, for example, Ezekiel, when the prophet is addressed by God as 'son of man', the phrase means little more than 'man', but man in his littleness as compared with the greatness of the God who is speaking to him.

It is worthy of note that, apart from Acts 7.56, Jesus is the only one who uses the phrase–no one else is ever recorded as using it with reference to him. Perhaps this indicates that he thought of himself–and wanted others to think of him–as one of the sons of men, like them in his humanity, one who has been made like us in order that he may make us like God, indeed sons of God.

If it is legitimate to think along these lines in interpreting this phrase, we are getting close to that concept of the servant of the Lord which has occupied us over the last two days.

The two passages chosen for today's reading illustrate the two nuances of the phrase–the Son of Man so poor and humble that he has no place to lay his head, and the Son of Man sending out his angels at the end of time.

Since all he comes to ransom,
By all be he adored,
The infant born in Bethlehem,
The Saviour and the Lord.

LENT 2 Friday

READING John 1.1–14

When all things began, the Word already was. The Word dwelt with God, and what
God was, the Word was. [2]The Word, then, was with God at the beginning, [3]and
through him all things came to be; no single thing was created without him. All that
came to be [4]was alive with his life, and that life was the light of men. [5]The light shines
on in the dark, and the darkness has never mastered it.
[6]There appeared a man named John, sent from God; [7]he came as a witness to
testify to the light, that all might become believers through him. [8]He was not himself
the light; he came to bear witness to the light. [9]The real light which enlightens every
man was even then coming into the world.
[10]He was in the world; but the world, though it owed its being to him, did not
recognize him. [11]He entered his own realm, and his own would not receive him.
[12]But to all who did receive him, to those who have yielded him their allegiance,
he gave the right to become children of God, [13]not born of any human stock, or by
the fleshly desire of a human father, but the offspring of God himself. [14]So the
Word became flesh; he came to dwell among us, and we saw his glory, such glory
as befits the Father's only Son, full of grace and truth.

WORD

There is something mysterious, even miraculous, about a word. Words are conveyors. They are the means by which a thought in my mind is conveyed to your mind. If I say the word 'war', you see the slaughter and bloodshed which I also saw when I uttered the word. If I say 'I love you', something in the emotional part of me is conveyed to you–heart speaks to heart, as we say.

When St John was seeking to find the most effective way of telling his readers what happened when Jesus was born, he could have used a variety of expressions. He might, for example, have spoken of Jesus as the Wisdom of God, for such passages as Proverbs 8 had prepared men to think in those terms. But he by-passed that concept and chose to speak of Jesus as the word of God. Why? Because Jesus conveyed in his own person, as no other had done, what was in the mind and on the heart of God–what God wanted to say to men because he loved them.

God had, in a limited way, done that already through the prophets, conveying something of his justice through the words of an Amos and of his love through the words of a Hosea. But such revelation was necessarily partial. When Christ came, there was in him such an exposure of the mind and heart of God as men had never been granted before. Here was the Word enfleshed, incarnate, dwelling among us . . . full of grace and truth.

When Bishop Lancelot Andrewes thought of the Babe of Bethlehem, he spoke of him as 'the Word, yet unable to speak a word'. Let us meditate on that–and wonder–and worship.

LENT 2 Saturday

READING John 6.30–35

They said, 'What sign can you give us to see, so that we may believe you? What is the
work you do? [31]Our ancestors had manna to eat in the desert; as Scripture
says, "He gave them bread from heaven to eat." ' [32]Jesus answered, 'I tell you this:
the truth is, not that Moses gave you the bread from heaven, but that my Father
gives you the real bread from heaven. [33]The bread that God gives comes down
from heaven and brings life to the world.' [34]They said to him, 'Sir, give us this
bread now and always.' [35]Jesus said to them, 'I am the bread of life. Whoever
comes to me shall never be hungry, and whoever believes in me shall never be
thirsty.'

BREAD

In the coming eight days we shall be considering the series of claims which the evangelist depicts Jesus as making. They all begin with the two words 'I am', and describe some aspect of our Lord's work as the Word made flesh.

The words 'I am' in the setting of this Gospel are suggestive of deity. When Moses asked God what answer he should give to those who inquired what God's name was, God replied: 'I am who I am . . . This is my name for all time' (Exodus 3.13–15). Jewish readers, considering this series of claims beginning with the words 'I am', would almost inevitably have thought back to the passage which spoke of the revelation of the divine name to Moses. That revelation is fulfilled in Jesus, and its meaning is elaborated in the series of claims and in the discourses at whose heart they occur.

Our Lord's claim to be the bread of life is set in the middle of a debate about the story of provision of food for the hungry and grumbling Israelites during their journey in the wilderness (Exodus 16). God had, through Moses, met their need. But need and provision were alike transitory. The bread which Jesus in his own person supplies is the true, real bread which issues not in the satisfaction of a passing appetite but in life which is everlasting. To believe on him, to yield him allegiance, results in no more hunger, no more thirst. 'The man who comes to me I will never turn away' (v.37).

I hunger and I thirst:
Jesu, my manna be.

Thou bruised and broken Bread,
My life-long wants supply;
As living souls are fed,
O feed me, or I die.

LENT 3 Monday

READING John 9.1–7

As he went on his way Jesus saw a man blind from his birth. [2]His disciples put the
question, 'Rabbi, who sinned, this man or his parents? Why was he born blind?' [3]'It
is not that this man or his parents sinned,' Jesus answered; 'he was born blind so that
God's power might be displayed in curing him. [4]While daylight lasts we must carry
on the work of him who sent me; night comes, when no one can work. [5]While I am
in the world I am the light of the world.'

[6]With these words he spat on the ground and made a paste with the spittle; he
spread it on the man's eyes, [7]and said to him, 'Go and wash in the pool of Siloam.'
(The name means 'sent'.) The man went away and washed, and when he returned
he could see.

LIGHT

The claims of Jesus to be the light of the world had been made in John 8.12. Here it is worked out in the context of a story of the giving of sight to a man born blind.

In his reply to the disciples' question, Jesus strikes a blow at the doctrine that physical disease is necessarily the result of sin, either on the part of the man or of his parents. Greek manuscripts had practically no punctuation; so it is possible to read vv.3 and 4 thus: 'Neither this man sinned nor his parents. But that the works of God may be manifested in him, we must work the works of him who sent me while it is day . . .'

The whole chapter should be read, for it depicts a scene of pathetic blindness–spiritual, not physical–on the part of the neighbours (vv.8–12), the Pharisees (vv.13–17) and the Jews generally (vv.18ff). The Jews had enjoyed the privilege of receiving the Law of God, and were the heirs of the prophets who spoke of him. Yet they were blind to the supreme revelation of God in Christ. 'A man who is unspiritual refuses what belongs to the Spirit of God; it is folly to him; he cannot grasp it . . .' (1 Corinthians 2.14).

The man who was cured had not got the theological 'know-how' to be able to engage in deep debate with the religious people of his day. He could only say: 'All I know is this: once I was blind, now I can see' (v.25). There is no getting round such a testimony.

To thy Name, Lord Jesus, help me to
bow the knee and all its worshipping;
bow the head and all its thinking;
bow the will and all its choosing;
bow the heart and all its loving,
today, tomorrow, and all the days of my life.

LENT 3 Tuesday

READING John 10.1–10

'In truth I tell you, in very truth, the man who does not enter the sheepfold by the
door, but climbs in some other way, is nothing but a thief or a robber. 2The man who
enters by the door is the shepherd in charge of the sheep. 3The door-keeper admits
him, and the sheep hear his voice; he calls his own sheep by name, and leads them
out. 4When he has brought them all out, he goes ahead and the sheep follow,
because they know his voice. 5They will not follow a stranger; they will run away
from him, because they do not recognize the voice of strangers.'

6This was a parable that Jesus told them, but they did not understand what he
meant by it.

7So Jesus spoke again: 'In truth, in very truth I tell you, I am the door of the
sheepfold. 8The sheep paid no heed to any who came before me, for these were all
thieves and robbers. 9I am the door; anyone who comes into the fold through me
shall be safe. He shall go in and out and shall find pasturage.

10'The thief comes only to steal, to kill, to destroy; I have come that men may
have life, and may have it in all its fullness.'

DOOR

Jesus is both door (v.7) and shepherd (vv.11, 14). In a sense, door and shepherd fulfil the same function in eastern shepherding, for at night the shepherd would lay himself down at the entrance to the fold–any marauding beast must pass over his body before it could reach the sheep!

Probably Jesus had in mind the Pharisees when he referred to the thieves and robbers who stole and killed and destroyed. There were, of course, many Pharisees who, according to their lights, were godly religious leaders. But there were those who, by their insistence on the necessity of obedience to the minute details of the law, made religion a burden and robbed it of its joy and freedom. Such religion could only lead to death; Jesus came that men might have 'life in all its fullness'.

There is an exuberance about true Christianity which is self-authenticating. It was so obvious in some of the earliest disciples that their critics said, no doubt with a touch of contempt: 'They have been drinking!' (Acts 2.13). St Paul, great sufferer though he was and mighty wrestler with the powers of evil, often breaks out in his writings with exclamations, doxologies, of wonder and joy. He had 'life in all its fullness'.

If a complete outsider came into your church–or your home, for that matter–would this feature of Christianity quickly strike him?

If thus, good Lord, thy grace be given,
Our glory meets us *ere* we die;
Before we upward pass to heaven
We taste our immortality.

LENT 3 Wednesday

READING John 10.11–18

'I am the good shepherd; the good shepherd lays down his life for the sheep. [12]The
hireling, when he sees the wolf coming, abandons the sheep and runs away, because
he is no shepherd and the sheep are not his. Then the wolf harries the flock and
scatters the sheep. [13]The man runs away because he is a hireling and cares nothing
for the sheep.

[14]'I am the good shepherd; I know my own sheep and my sheep know me– [15]as
the Father knows me and I know the Father–and I lay down my life for the sheep.
[16]But there are other sheep of mine, not belonging to this fold, whom I must bring
in; and they too will listen to my voice. There will then be one flock, one shepherd.
[17]The Father loves me because I lay down my life, to receive it back again. [18]No one
has robbed me of it; I am laying it down of my own free will. I have the right to lay it
down, and I have the right to receive it back again: this charge I have received from
my Father.'

SHEPHERD

It is hard to imagine a more peaceful, pastoral scene than an English field, say in April, full of sheep and new-born lambs. Of course, we know that there has been hard work on the shepherd's part to make that possible, and some cold nights in the field when things have been difficult for the ewes. But one's mind rarely turns to the thought of *danger* when confronted by this idyllic scene. In the East in biblical times, things were different. David told Saul how, whenever a lion or a bear came out to harry the flock which he was shepherding, he would engage in a struggle with the beast (1 Samuel 17.34–37). Such struggles could, and no doubt on occasion did, lead to the death of the shepherd.

It is in the context of such grappling with evil that Jesus speaks of himself as shepherd of the sheep. He is the *good* shepherd, prepared, unlike the hired man, to lay down his life for the sheep, and to do so 'of his own free will', out of sheer love and care. His will is at one with his Father's, and he is prepared to go through with this rescue operation to the end.

Old Testament prophets had often spoken of religious leaders who were more concerned for their own wealth and ease than for the welfare of their people; they were unfaithful shepherds (see, for example, Ezekiel 34). In Jesus we see the true shepherd, faithful unto death.

O God, whose Son Jesus is the good shepherd of your people: Grant that when we hear his voice we may know him who calls us each by name, and follow where he leads; who, with you and the Holy Spirit, lives and reigns, one God, for ever and ever.

LENT 3 Thursday

READING John 14.1–6

'Set your troubled hearts at rest. Trust in God always; trust also in me. [2]There are
many dwelling-places in my Father's house; if it were not so I should have told you;
for I am going there on purpose to prepare a place for you. [3]And if I go and prepare
a place for you, I shall come again and receive you to myself, so that where I am you
may be also; [4]and my way there is known to you.' [5]Thomas said.'Lord, we do not
know where you are going, so how can we know the way?' [6]Jesus replied, 'I am the
way; I am the truth and I am life; no one comes to the Father except by me.'

WAY

We shall leave over the claim of Jesus, 'I am the resurrection' (John 11.25) for Easter Day, and in the next three days think about his claim to be the way, the truth and the life.

'I am the *way*.' Thomas's frank question 'How can we know the way?'–the way to the Father, to eternal life–has been echoed by multitudes down the centuries, and is echoed today. Thomas found the answer in his own experience only after deep travail (see John 20.24–29). Another seeker, Saul of Tarsus, thought the answer was to be found in a life of strict religious orthodoxy. But he found that that road was marked 'No way through'. Then he met Christ. Looking back on that meeting and the liberation of spirit which followed it, he wrote: 'Through Christ we have access to God–with freedom–in the confidence born of trust in him' (Ephesians 3.12). He had found Christ to be the way (see also Romans 5.2).

Hence the urgency of Christ's bidding in v.1–'Trust in God always; trust also in me'. That is the only way in which 'troubled hearts' can be 'set at rest'. It is like a swimmer who abandons his wild attempts with arms flailing to stay alive in the water, and, ceasing from such effort, finds that the water carries him.

Almighty Father, whom truly to know is eternal life, teach us to know your Son Jesus Christ as the *way*, the truth and the life; that we may follow the steps of your holy apostles, and walk steadfastly in the way that leads to your glory; through Jesus Christ our Lord.

LENT 3 Friday

READING John 14.6–10

Jesus replied, 'I am the way; I am the truth and I am life; no one comes to the Father except by me.

[7]'If you knew me you would know my Father too. From now on you do know him; you have seen him.' [8]Philip said to him, 'Lord, show us the Father and we ask no more.' [9]Jesus answered, 'Have I been all this time with you, Philip, and you still do not know me? Anyone who has seen me has seen the Father. Then how can you say, "Show us the Father"? [10]Do you not believe that I am the Father, and the Father in me? I am not myself the source of the words I speak to you; it is the Father who dwells in me doing his own work.'

TRUTH

'I am the *truth*'. The context of this tremendous claim makes it clear that the truth about which Jesus is speaking is the knowledge of God *as Father*. When he says 'no one comes to the Father except by me', he means that if you want to know God *as Father*, then he who is the truth must teach you.

Professor Jeremias has made a very strong case for the view that our Lord's invocation of God as *Abba*, Father, is unique–'nowhere in the literature of the prayers of ancient Judaism . . . is this invocation of God as *Abba* to be found'. Here is one who speaks with his father simply, intimately, securely. Jesus then shared this insight, this revelation, with his chosen disciples–they too could share in his close communion with God. *And they did*. In a passage which probably reflects a baptism scene, St Paul depicts the new-born sons of God doing what the Son of God had done, and crying out, as he cried out, '*Abba*, Daddy, Father' (Romans 8.14–17).

Such knowledge of God as Father is not an intellectual achievement, though loving God with the mind is an essential part of Christian discipleship. Rather, it comes through faith. And 'faith', to quote Jeremias again, 'is not an achievement in itself, rather it is the hand which grasps the work of Christ and holds it out to God'.

Almighty Father, whom truly to know is eternal life, teach us to know your Son Jesus Christ as the way, the *truth* and the life; that we may follow the steps of your holy apostles, and walk steadfastly in the way that leads to your glory; through Jesus Christ our Lord.

LENT 3 Saturday

READING John 14.22–26

Judas asked him–the other Judas, not Iscariot–'Lord, what can have happened, that you mean to disclose yourself to us alone and not to the world?' [23]Jesus replied, 'Anyone who loves me will heed what I say; then my Father will love him, and we will come to him and make our dwelling with him; [24]but he who does not love me does not heed what I say. And the word you hear is not mine: it is the word of the Father who sent me. [25]I have told you all this while I am still here with you; [26]but your Advocate, the Holy Spirit whom the Father will send in my name, will teach you everything, and will call to mind all that I have told you.'

LIFE

'I am *life*'. 'Life' in the New Testament means more than physical life. Nor is it life after death only. Eternal life begins in the here and now, and is of such a quality that it is inconceivable that the physical incident of death should terminate it.

This claim of Jesus to be life should be read together with the great prologue to this Gospel (1.1–18). The writer describes the Word as the source of all life–'All that came to be was alive with his life, and that life was the light of men'. The theme is taken up again in chapter 3, where spiritual life is spoken of in terms of a new birth, and the purpose of God's sending his Son is said to be that we may not die but have eternal life (3.16). This life is offered to those who 'receive' Christ, who yield him their allegiance (1.12), who, in the words of today's passage, love him and heed what he says (14.23).

Such people become a dwelling-place for God. Such people are in a position to be taught by his Spirit (v.26), the Advocate, the Counsellor, the one who comes to stand by us, the stimulator of mind and conscience, the intercessor.

When that happens, there is no limit to the abundance of life which is ours–*and* it is 'life that shall endless be'. The Christian is the heir to the best of both worlds!

Almighty Father, whom truly to know is eternal life; teach us to know your Son Jesus Christ as the way, the truth and the *life*; that we may follow the steps of your holy apostles, and walk steadfastly in the way that leads to your glory; through Jesus Christ our Lord.

LENT 4 Monday

READING John 15.1–10

'I am the real vine and my Father is the gardener. 2Every barren branch of mine he
cuts away; and every fruiting branch he cleans, to make it more fruitful still. 3You
have already been cleansed by the word that I spoke to you. 4Dwell in me, as I in
you. No branch can bear fruit by itself, but only if it remains united with the vine; no
more can you bear fruit, unless you remain united with me.

5'I am the vine, and you the branches. He who dwells in me, as I dwell in him,
bears much fruit; for apart from me you can do nothing. 6He who does not dwell in
me is thrown away like a withered branch. The withered branches are heaped
together, thrown on the fire, and burnt.

7'If you dwell in me, and my words dwell in you, ask what you will, and you shall
have it. 8This is my Father's glory, that you may bear fruit in plenty and so be my
disciples. 9As the Father has loved me, so I have loved you. Dwell in my love.
10If you heed my commands, you will dwell in my love, as I have heeded my Father's
commands and dwell in his love.'

VINE

Israel is often compared in the Old Testament to a vine–read, for example, the opening verses of Isaiah 5 where the prophet complains that the nation has not responded to the Lord's nurture–it has 'yielded wild grapes'. Jesus is the real, true, faithful vine, who makes a response of total faithfulness to the Father. The disciples who dwell in him are the true Israel, bringing forth abundant fruit.

Mrs Hamilton King catches St John's meaning well in her poem *The Disciples*:

'The Living Vine, Christ chose it for himself;
God gave to man for use and sustenance
Corn, wine and oil, and each of these is good
And Christ is Bread of Life, and Light of Life.
But yet he did not choose the summer corn,
That shoots up straight and free in one quick growth,
And has its day, and is done, and springs no more:
Nor yet the olive, all whose boughs are spread
In the soft air, and never lose a leaf,
Flowering and fruitful in perpetual peace:
But only this for him and his in one–
The everlasting, ever-quickening Vine,
That gives the heat and passion of the world,
Through its own life-blood, still renewed and shed.'

The lesson is clear:

'Measure thy life by loss instead of gain;
Not by the wine drunk, but the wine poured forth;

For love's strength standeth in love's sacrifice;
And whoso suffers most hath most to give.'

To thy Name, Lord Jesus, help me to
bow the knee and all its worshipping;
bow the head and all its thinking;
bow the will and all its choosing;
bow the heart and all its loving,
today, tomorrow, and all the days of my life.

LENT 4 Tuesday

READING Revelation 1.1–5

This is the Revelation given by God to Jesus Christ. It was given to him so that he might show his servants what must shortly happen. He made it known by sending his angel to his servant John, [2]who, in telling all that he saw, has borne witness to the word of God and to the testimony of Jesus Christ.

[3]Happy is the man who reads, and happy those who listen to the words of this prophecy and heed what is written in it. For the hour of fulfilment is near.

[4]John to the seven churches in the province of Asia.

Grace be to you and peace, from him who is and who was and who is to come, from the seven spirits before his throne, [5]and from Jesus Christ, the faithful witness, the first-born from the dead and ruler of the kings of the earth.

FAITHFUL WITNESS

We have spent the last nine days in considering facets of our Lord's person and work given to us in St John's Gospel. We shall spend the rest of this week in doing the same thing, but drawing on the opening chapters of the Book of the Revelation.

This book was written by a man who himself was a refugee, expelled from his own country to Patmos (probably to work in the mines) because he had preached God's word and borne his testimony to Jesus (1.9). As he wrote, he had particularly in mind those who, like himself, were being persecuted for their faith. As we shall see, his descriptions of our Lord are particularly meaningful to such people.

In v.5 Jesus Christ is described as the faithful witness. The writer, in bearing his own witness (vv.2, 9), was following in the steps of Christ himself whose witness had been totally faithful, even unto death. Jesus had testified to this before Pilate: 'My task is to bear witness to the truth. For this was I born; for this I came into the world . . .' (John 18.37).

The picture of Jesus as the faithful witness, which the writer of the Revelation holds up to his readers, must have been a source of immense strength to them. It certainly was to Bonhoeffer, in a Nazi prison because he bore witness to the word of God. It is to thousands in Soviet prison camps or Latin American gaols–and to many nearer home. What does *our* witness to the truth as we see it cost *us*?

> 'You will receive power when the Holy Spirit comes upon you; and you will bear witness for me in Jerusalem, and all over Judaea and Samaria, and away to the ends of the earth' (Acts 1.8).

LENT 4 Wednesday

READING Revelation 1.4–8

John to the seven churches in the province of Asia.
Grace be to you and peace, from him who is and who was and who is to come,
from the seven spirits before his throne, 5and from Jesus Christ, the faithful witness,
the first-born from the dead and ruler of the kings of the earth.
To him who loves us and freed us from our sins with his life's blood, 6who made of
us a royal house, to serve as the priests of his God and Father–to him be glory and
dominion for ever and ever! Amen.
7Behold, he is coming with the clouds! Every eye shall see him, and among them
those who pierced him; and all the peoples of the world shall lament in remorse. So
it shall be. Amen.
8'I am the Alpha and the Omega', says the Lord God, who is and who was and
who is to come, the sovereign Lord of all.

FIRST-BORN FROM THE DEAD

The Christian Church, in the days when the Revelation was written, was a tiny minority movement. To bear witness to Jesus in one of those towns in Asia Minor or, still more, among the deportees on Patmos, must have been a horribly lonely experience. Those Christians must have felt alone–yet they were not alone. Christ was risen! That knowledge bore them up, and hearts were brave again and arms were strong.

They did not bear witness to a dead Christ. He was 'the first-born from the dead'. St Paul had used that phrase (Colossians 1.18). If he was the first-born, that was the guarantee that they themselves were sons and daughters of the resurrection. Using a slightly different metaphor, St Paul had spoken of Christ raised from the dead as 'the first-fruits' of a mighty harvest (1 Corinthians 15.20). Jesus, their elder brother, the first-born, the first-fruits, was alive!

This writer went even further. Looking across the sea from the little island of Patmos to the great world dominated by the Roman Emperor, he might have felt overawed and overwhelmed by that terrible domination. Not so. Jesus Christ–he knew it by faith–was not only 'the first-born from the dead'. He was also 'ruler of the kings of the earth' (v.5). The glory that was Rome had within it the seeds of decay. The kingdom of Christ was imperishable, for it was founded on love.

So be it, Lord; thy throne shall never,
Like earth's proud empires, pass away;
Thy Kingdom stands, and grows for ever,
Till all thy creatures own thy sway.

LENT 4 Thursday

READING Revelation 1.9–18

I, John, your brother, who share with you in the suffering and the sovereignty and
the endurance which is ours in Jesus–I was on the island called Patmos because I
had preached God's word and borne my testimony to Jesus. [10]It was on the Lord's
day, and I was caught up by the Spirit; and behind me I heard a loud voice, like the
sound of a trumpet, [11]which said to me, 'Write down what you see on a scroll and
send it to the seven churches: to Ephesus, Smyrna, Pergamum, Thyatira, Sardis,
Philadelphia, and Laodicea.' [12]I turned to see whose voice it was that spoke to me;
and when I turned I saw seven standing lamps of gold, [13]and among the lamps one
like a son of man, robed down to his feet, with a golden girdle round his breast.
[14]The hair of his head was white as snow-white wool, and his eyes flamed like fire;
[15]his feet gleamed like burnished brass refined in a furnace, and his voice was like
the sound of rushing waters. [16]In his right hand he held seven stars, and out of his
mouth came a sharp two-edged sword; and his face shone like the sun in full
strength.

[17]When I saw him, I fell at his feet as though dead. But he laid his right hand upon
me and said, 'Do not be afraid. I am the first and the last, [18]and I am the living one;
for I was dead and now I am alive for evermore, and I hold the keys of Death and
Death's domain.'

HOLDER OF THE KEYS

Sunday morning on Patmos! How this lonely refugee must have longed for eucharistic fellowship with other believers away on the mainland! He was given something even more wonderful than that. He was given a vision of Christ himself.

Language is strained in an attempt to convey something of the majesty of the one who spoke to him. The description owes much to the portrait of the Ancient of Days given in Daniel 7.9ff. Purity, omniscience, power–all are here. No wonder that the Seer 'fell in a dead faint at his feet' (v.17, Jerusalem Bible)! This vision makes our hand-shaking familiarity with God look rather small.

Reassurance comes to him as he finds a hand laid on him and hears a voice which bids him not to be afraid. The speaker claims to be 'the first and the last', sharing the attributes of God most high; once dead, but now alive for evermore (see yesterday's notes); and now holding the keys that unlock death and Hades (the abode where departed spirits were conceived of as awaiting final judgement). This authority has been won by Christ through his own death.

In the assurance of Christ's victory over death the Christian finds victory over fear. Even martyrdom is merely the prelude to complete fellowship with him who says: 'Do not be afraid . . . I hold the keys'.

> The Lord is my light and my salvation; whom then shall I fear?
> The Lord is the strength of my life; of whom then shall I be afraid?
> (Psalm 27.1)

LENT 4 Friday

READING Revelation 5.1–10

Then I saw in the right hand of the One who sat on the throne a scroll, with writing
inside and out, and it was sealed up with seven seals. [2]And I saw a mighty angel
proclaiming in a loud voice, 'Who is worthy to open the scroll and to break its seals?'
[3]There was no one in heaven or on earth or under the earth able to open the scroll or
to look inside it. [4]I was in tears because no one was found who was worthy to open
the scroll or to look inside it. [5]But one of the elders said to me: 'Do not weep; for the
Lion from the tribe of Judah, the Scion of David, has won the right to open the
scroll and break its seven seals.'

[6]Then I saw standing in the very middle of the throne, inside the circle of living
creatures and the circle of elders, a Lamb with the marks of slaughter upon him. He
had seven horns and seven eyes, the eyes which are the seven spirits of God sent out
over all the world. [7]And the Lamb went up and took the scroll from the right hand
of the One who sat on the throne. [8]When he took it, the four living creatures and the
twenty-four elders fell down before the Lamb. Each of the elders had a harp, and
they held golden bowls full of incense, the prayers of God's people, [9]and they were
singing a new song:

> 'Thou art worthy to take the scroll and to break its seals, for thou wast slain and by
> thy blood didst purchase for God men of every tribe and language, people
> and nation; [10]thou hast made of them a royal house, to serve our God as priests; and
> they shall reign upon earth.'

LAMB

What an extraordinary picture we are given here! A scroll sealed with seven seals, or, as we should say, a problem insoluble by human ingenuity. Faced with that, one of the elders tells the Seer that the Lion from the tribe of Judah has won the right to open the scroll. We wait to see the *Lion* appear, the king of beasts. We wait in vain. A *Lamb* appears–with the marks of slaughter upon it. True, it has seven horns (power). True, it has seven eyes (knowledge). But a Lamb it is, symbolizing meekness and gentleness, sacrifice and suffering unto death. Here is power indeed, but power interpreted in terms of gentleness and sacrifice; and this it is which prevails.

What does this scroll represent? Is it the Old Testament, sealed till Jesus opens it (see Luke 24.27)? Is it the hidden Name of God? Is it the *why* of a suffering world and of a persecuted Church? Is it mankind's long, deep hunger for meaning–a hunger fully satisfied only in Christ, the Lamb of God, the Word of God who has made him known (John 1.18)? The Seer gives no exclusive answer; he leaves the reader free to think this out for himself.

It is significant that this description of Jesus as the Lamb is the Seer's favourite description. It occurs no less than twenty-eight times in this book. It would be a worthwhile study to look out these occurrences–they provide a galaxy of descriptions, each one of which is deserving of our thought.

> 'Worthy is the Lamb, the Lamb that was slain, to receive all power and wealth, wisdom and might, honour and glory and praise!' (Revelation 5.12).

LENT 4 Saturday

READING Revelation 22.16–21

'I, Jesus, have sent my angel to you with this testimony for the churches. I am the
scion and offspring of David, the bright star of dawn.'
17 'Come!' say the Spirit and the bride.
'Come!' let each hearer reply.
Come forward, you who are thirsty; accept the water of life, a free gift to all
who desire it.
18 For my part, I give this warning to everyone who is listening to the words of
prophecy in this book: should anyone add to them, God will add to him the plagues
described in this book; 19 should anyone take away from the words in this book of
prophecy, God will take away from him his share in the tree of life and the Holy
City, described in this book.
20 He who gives this testimony speaks: 'Yes, I am coming soon!'
Amen. Come, Lord Jesus!
21 The grace of the Lord Jesus be with you all.

BRIGHT STAR OF DAWN

The Jews were looking for a 'scion and offspring of David'–had not Isaiah said: 'A shoot shall grow from the stock of Jesse, and a branch shall spring from his roots' (Isaiah 11.1)? They were awaiting a 'bright star of dawn'–had not the book of Numbers said: 'A star shall come forth out of Jacob, a comet arise from Israel' (Numbers 24.17)? Now his followers knew that in Christ this scion, this star, had arrived.

Jesus inaugurated a new era of light to penetrate and to succeed the darkness of the world. As St John wrote in the preface to his Gospel: 'The light shines on in the dark, and the darkness has never mastered it' (1.5). Even on Patmos, among the refugees working in the mines, the light shone. It was like the bright star which was a sure token that the dawn and the full blaze of day would not long be delayed.

Strengthened by this hope of the ultimate victory of Christ's cause, the Church goes on its way, witnessing in the darkest places and issuing its invitation to anyone who will listen–'*come*' (v.17). It is a divine invitation, given by the Spirit of God himself. He issues that invitation with and through the Church, here called the Bride (that is, the Bride of Christ, the Lamb–so described in 21.9). Only in response to that invitation will man's thirst for truth, for life, for reality be satisfied. All who want may have this water of life, but they must be humble enough to realize that it is theirs for the taking, *free*; it cannot be earned.

I heard the voice of Jesus say,
'Behold, I freely give
The living water, thirsty one;
Stoop down and drink and live'.

LENT 5 Monday

READING 1 Timothy 1.1–2, 15–17

From Paul, apostle of Christ Jesus by command of God our Saviour and Christ Jesus our hope, [2]to Timothy his true-born son in the faith.

Grace, mercy, and peace to you from God the Father and Christ Jesus our Lord.

[15]Here are words you may trust, words that merit full acceptance: 'Christ
Jesus came into the world to save sinners'; and among them I stand first. [16]But I was
mercifully dealt with for this very purpose, that Jesus Christ might find in me the
first occasion for displaying all his patience, and that I might be typical of all who
were in future to have faith in him and gain eternal life. [17]Now to the King of all
worlds, immortal, invisible, the only God, be honour and glory for ever and ever!
Amen.

OUR HOPE

It is a short step from thinking of Christ as 'the bright star of dawn', as we did on Saturday, to thinking of him as 'our hope' (v.1). St Paul spoke of 'Christ in you (or, among you), the hope of a glory to come' (Colossians 1.27).

What is the Christian's ultimate hope? The New Testament is clear as to the answer. It is this: man was made in the image of God. This image has been defaced and marred by sin (Romans 3.23). His hope–sure and certain–is that that image will be restored. That is his 'glory'. We 'exult in the hope of the divine splendour that is to be ours' (Romans 5.2). In the words of St John, 'we shall be like him, because we shall see him as he is' (1 John 3.2). When 'our Lord Jesus Christ appears' (1 Timothy 6.14), the salvation of which we now enjoy a foretaste will be bestowed in full measure.

On a vaster scale, the reign of God, inaugurated with the coming of Christ to this earth, will be consummated. At present, 'we see not yet all things put under him' (Hebrews 2.8 AV)–that is all too obvious and all too true! But faith looks to the day when Christ shall reign and all enemies be put under his feet. That is the specifically Christian hope, which nothing can destroy. Whatever the future of our little world may be, even if man in his folly destroys it, the ultimate victory of God is assured, and he has given a pledge of it in the resurrection of his Son.

To thy Name, Lord Jesus, help me to
  bow the knee and all its worshipping;
  bow the head and all its thinking;
  bow the will and all its choosing;
  bow the heart and all its loving,
today, tomorrow, and all the days of my life.

LENT 5 Tuesday

READING 2 Corinthians 5.1–10

For we know that if the earthly frame that houses us today should be demolished,
we possess a building which God has provided–a house not made by human hands,
eternal, and in heaven. 2In this present body we do indeed groan; we yearn to have
our heavenly habitation put on over this one–3in the hope that, being thus clothed,
we shall not find ourselves naked. 4We groan indeed, we who are enclosed within
this earthly frame; we are oppressed because we do not want to have the old body
stripped off. Rather our desire is to have the new body put on over it, so that our
mortal part may be absorbed into life immortal. 5God himself has shaped us for this
very end; and as a pledge of it he has given us the Spirit.
6Therefore we never cease to be confident. We know that so long as we are at
home in the body we are exiles from the Lord; 7faith is our guide, we do not see him.
8We are confident, I repeat, and would rather leave our home in the body and go to
live with the Lord. 9We therefore make it our ambition, wherever we are, here or
there, to be acceptable to him. 10For we must all have our lives laid open before the
tribunal of Christ, where each must receive what is due to him for his conduct in the
body, good or bad.

JUDGE

When anyone becomes a disciple of Jesus Christ, he finds himself deeply involved in the world around him. It cannot be otherwise, since his Lord became man, earned his living, cared deeply for the welfare of his contemporaries, mixed freely with people of all types. A Christian disciple has his duty to Caesar as well as to God. He is a *this*-worldly man.

But he is also an *other*-worldly man. He knows that when his earthly body is worn out, that is not the end of him. Far from it. His mortal body will 'be absorbed into life immortal' (v.4)–'God himself has shaped us for this very end.' He will 'go to live with the Lord' (v.8). That is his destiny, and the hope of it fills him with joy.

Read the New Testament, and you will see that what the theologians call 'the eschatological hope', that is, the expectation of the End, the consummation of all things, loomed large in the thought of the early Christians. Many of them got it wrong in that they expected it in the immediate future. That was a hope which was not realized. The miracle was that the Church survived that major disappointment. It is a pity that succeeding generations of Christians have got so entangled with the *when* of this hope, that their attention has often been distracted from the *fact* of what St Paul calls 'the tribunal of Christ' (v.10). This for a Christian is no cause for fear or terror, but it should sober him and nerve him for the fight. 'We must all have our lives laid open before the tribunal of Christ.'

Purify our conscience, Almighty God, by your daily visitation, that your Son Jesus Christ, at his coming, may find in us a mansion prepared for himself.

LENT 5 Wednesday

READING James 2.1–9

My brothers, believing as you do in our Lord Jesus Christ, who reigns in glory, you
must never show snobbery. [2]For instance, two visitors may enter your place of
worship, one a well-dressed man with gold rings, and the other a poor man in
shabby clothes. [3]Suppose you pay special attention to the well-dressed man and say
to him, 'Please take this seat', while to the poor man you say, 'You can stand; or you
may sit here on the floor by my footstool', [4]do you not see that you are inconsistent
and judge by false standards?
[5]Listen, my friends. Has not God chosen those who are poor in the eyes of the
world to be rich in faith and to inherit the kingdom he has promised to those who
love him? [6]And yet you have insulted the poor man. Moreover, are not the rich your
oppressors? Is it not they who drag you into court [7]and pour contempt on the
honoured name by which God has claimed you?
[8]If, however, you are observing the sovereign law laid down in Scripture, 'Love
your neighbour as yourself', that is excellent. [9]But if you show snobbery, you are
committing a sin and you stand convicted by that law as transgressors.

THE GLORY

The Epistle of St James, so practical and down to earth, could almost have taken its place in the Old Testament were it not for its two distinct references to our Lord Jesus Christ (1.1; 2.1). The phrase in the latter is unusual, and the translations are mostly paraphrases–'our glorious Lord Jesus Christ' (Phillips); 'our Lord Jesus Christ who reigns in glory' (NEB). Strictly, it can be translated 'our Lord Jesus Christ, (who is) the glory'. Nowhere else in the New Testament is our Lord described exactly like this, but we might ask: if he can be spoken of as 'the Word', why should he not be spoken of as 'the glory'?

Isaiah spoke of God as man's glory–'the Lord shall be your everlasting light, your God shall be your glory' (60.19). And St Paul said that 'God . . . has shined in our hearts, to give the light of the knowledge of the *glory* of God *in the face of Jesus Christ* (2 Corinthians 4.6 AV). So we need not be too surprised when we find St James speaking of Christ as 'the glory'.

The phrase forms the opening of a very pointed denunciation of snobbery, and of a searching contrast between the poor who are rich in faith (v.5) and the poor little rich men who lord it over those they think of as less fortunate than themselves. How wrong can we be?

Of Christ crucified, risen and ascended, the *Te Deum* says: 'Thou art the King of Glory, O Christ'. Come, let us worship him.

There was a time when Jesus had to rebuke Peter. 'You stand right in my path, Peter, when you look at things from man's point of view and not from God's' (Matthew 16.23 Phillips).

LENT 5 Thursday

READING Hebrews 1.1–4

When in former times God spoke to our forefathers, he spoke in fragmentary and varied fashion through the prophets. [2]But in this the final age he has spoken to us in the Son whom he has made heir to the whole universe, and through whom he created all orders of existence: [3]the Son who is the effulgence of God's splendour and the stamp of God's very being, and sustains the universe by his word of power. When he had brought about the purgation of sins, he took his seat at the right hand of Majesty on high, [4]raised as far above the angels, as the title he has inherited is superior to theirs.

SON OF GOD

The Epistle to the Hebrews is very rich in the facets of our Lord's person which it gives us. Small wonder–for it was written to Christian minority groups who were undergoing persecution for Christ's sake, and the best source of strength for them was undoubtedly to 'consider him' (3.1; 12.3 AV). So, up to and including Good Friday, we shall turn to this book.

The first chapter should be read as a whole, though the first four verses give us the gist of what the writer wants to say. It has parallels to the prologue to St John, and they are worth noting.

Because God is love, he is the God who speaks. Love cannot remain silent. It must find expression. God's love for his world expressed itself in the sending of a series of prophets, each of whom spoke of some particular aspect of God–Isaiah and Amos of his justice, Hosea of his yearning love, and so on. They spoke–and were rejected. 'Last of all', as the parable puts it, 'he sent to them his son' (Matthew 21.37).

The Son is described in terms of cosmic greatness–'through him he created all orders of existence'; 'he sustains the universe by his word of power'. He is the *ascended* Christ, 'seated at the right hand of Majesty on high'. The resurrection is assumed; the ascension is elaborated. Yet it is Christ in his oneness with us and his nearness to us of which this remarkable book constantly speaks, as we shall see in the coming days.

'This is my beloved Son: hear him.'

LENT 5 Friday

READING Hebrews 2.10–18

It was clearly fitting that God for whom and through whom all things exist should, in
bringing many sons to glory, make the leader who delivers them perfect through
sufferings. 11For a consecrating priest and those whom he consecrates are all of one
stock; and that is why the Son does not shrink from calling men his brothers, 12when
he says, 'I will proclaim thy name to my brothers; in full assembly I will sing thy
praise'; 13and again, 'I will keep my trust fixed on him'; and again, 'Here am I, and
the children whom God has given me.' 14The children of a family share the same
flesh and blood; and so he too shared ours, so that through death he might break the
power of him who had death at his command, that is, the devil; 15and might liberate
those who, through fear of death, had all their lifetime been in servitude. 16It is not
angels, mark you, that he takes to himself, but the sons of Abraham. 17And
therefore he had to be made like these brothers of his in every way, so that he might
be merciful and faithful as their high priest before God, to expiate the sins of the
people. 18For since he himself has passed through the test of suffering, he is able to
help those who are meeting their test now.

BROTHER

It comes to us naturally to think of Jesus in terms of grandeur–God's Anointed, God's Son, Emmanuel, etc. But to think of him as our brother–*my* brother–this is enough to give us pause. And yet this is the theme which the writer elaborates here.

Jesus embarked on a great mission–'to bring many sons to glory' (v.10). To do this he must become one of them, and this included suffering as a necessary part of the work. So he shared our very flesh and blood–this writer refers frequently to the true *humanity* of Jesus, as we shall see. He even shared that experience of death which is a part of our common humanity. In doing so, he broke its power; he liberated us (vv.10, 15).

The writer had good authority for writing thus boldly about Jesus as our brother. St Mark records a moving incident about his mother and brothers wanting to see him when he was engaged presumably in teaching a crowd of people. He took the opportunity of speaking to them of a wider family, the family of those who do the will of God. 'Whoever does the will of God is my brother, my sister, my mother' (Mark 3.31–35).

Such a relationship to Christ has deep implications for our relationship to our brothers and sisters in Christ. There is the essence of the doctrine of the Church here.

He 'does not shrink from calling men his brothers' (v.11). Do we shrink from acknowledging him before men? Or from acknowledging his brethren, some of them despised and persecuted, as ours?

LENT 5 Saturday

READING Hebrews 3.1–6

Therefore, brothers in the family of God, who share a heavenly calling, think of the
Apostle and High Priest of the religion we profess, [2]who was faithful to God
who appointed him. Moses also was faithful in God's household; [3]and Jesus, of
whom I speak, has been deemed worthy of greater honour than Moses, as the
founder of a house enjoys more honour than his household. [4]For every house has its
founder; and the founder of all is God. [5]Moses, then, was faithful as a servitor in
God's whole household; his task was to bear witness to the words that God would
speak; [6]but Christ is faithful as a son, set over his household. And we are that
household of his, if only we are fearless and keep our hope high.

APOSTLE

In this passage, Jesus is thought of as brother (v.1–we are 'brothers in the family of God' *because* he is our brother), *High Priest* (we shall think about this on Good Friday) and *Son* (we considered that on Thursday). But he is also spoken of as *Apostle* (v.1). This writer was the only New Testament writer to use this noun in reference to Jesus.

We think of our Lord as the *sender*–he commissions us to service of various kinds. But an apostle is one who *is sent*, and Jesus was just that too–'as the Father sent me (literally, *apostled* me), so I send you' (John 20.21). Ours is an inherited apostleship; because the Father sent him, he sends us. And *as* the Father sent him, he sends us–to be bread to the hungry, light to those in darkness, shepherd to those who stray, life to those who are dead in sins.

The outstanding mark of Christ's apostleship was his faithfulness to God who appointed him (v.2). 'I do always those things that please him'–Jesus alone could make such a claim (John 8.29 AV). But we can at least make this our aim. We are likely to come near fulfilling that aim only if we keep *thinking* of our Apostle and High Priest (v.1). To fill your mind with the image of him is to begin to learn how, in your turn, you become an apostle.

O Lord God, who hast called thy servants to ventures of which we cannot see the ending, by paths as yet untrodden, through perils unknown: Give us faith to go out with a good courage, not knowing whither we go, but only that thy hand is leading us and thy love supporting us; to the glory of thy name.

HOLY WEEK Monday

READING Hebrews 5.1–10

For every high priest is taken from among men and appointed their representative before God, to offer gifts and sacrifices for sins. [2]He is able to bear patiently with the ignorant and erring, since he too is beset by weakness; [3]and because of this he is bound to make sin-offerings for himself no less than for the people. [4]And nobody arrogates the honour to himself: he is called by God, as indeed Aaron was. [5]So it is with Christ: he did not confer upon himself the glory of becoming high priest; it was granted by God, who said to him, 'Thou art my Son; today I have begotten thee'; [6]as also in another place he says, 'Thou art a priest for ever, in the succession of Melchizedek.' [7]In the days of his earthly life he offered up prayers and petitions, with loud cries and tears, to God who was able to deliver him from the grave. Because of his humble submission his prayer was heard: [8]son though he was, he learned obedience in the school of suffering, [9]and, once perfected, became the source of eternal salvation for all who obey him, [10]named by God high priest in the succession of Melchizedek.

LEARNER

How fresh the writer of this book is? We think of Jesus as the sender; he thinks of him as the sent (see yesterday's notes). We think of Jesus as the teacher; he thinks of him as the learner. Here is another instance of the writer's emphasis on the true humanity of Jesus. Step by step, painfully and progressively, he had to *learn*–and to learn what obedience meant, obedience to the will of the Father as it was increasingly made known to him.

Verse 7 is surely a commentary on Gethsemane and Calvary; and v.8 a commentary on the home years at Nazareth and the public years of our Lord's ministry.

Learning through suffering–the Greeks had a pun for that theme. They said *pathos mathos*–suffering is learning; if you suffer, you learn. But they never anchored that truth to a person of flesh and blood, a true brother of mine, as this writer does. He went through that painful stretching process of learning, and he did so through suffering. That is why he understands. In his ascended life, he *knows*, because he *knew*. The leader has been made perfect through sufferings (2.10).

It would be helpful, this first weekday of Holy Week, to look up what St Luke says about the boyhood of Jesus (2.40, 51–52), and then to read today's passage as a commentary on it. 'Think of him', the learner; and go on thinking all through Holy Week!

To thy Name, Lord Jesus, help me to
 bow the knee and all its worshipping;
 bow the head and all its thinking;
 bow the will and all its choosing;
 bow the heart and all its loving,
today, tomorrow, and all the days of my life.

HOLY WEEK Tuesday

READING Hebrews 12.1–6

And what of ourselves? With all these witnesses to faith around us like a cloud, we must throw off every encumbrance, every sin to which we cling, and run with resolution the race for which we are entered, [2]our eyes fixed on Jesus, on whom faith depends from start to finish: Jesus who, for the sake of the joy that lay ahead of him, endured the cross, making light of its disgrace, and has taken his seat at the right hand of the throne of God.

[3]Think of him who submitted to such opposition from sinners: that will help you not to lose heart and grow faint. [4]In your struggle against sin, you have not yet resisted to the point of shedding your blood. [5]You have forgotten the text of Scripture which addresses you as sons and appeals to you in these words:

'My son, do not think lightly of the Lord's discipline,
nor lose heart when he corrects you;
[6]for the Lord disciplines those whom he loves;
he lays the rod on every son whom he acknowledges.'

PIONEER

Verse 2 of this passage gives us two facets of the person and work of Jesus. The New English Bible translation is really a paraphrase: 'Jesus, on whom faith depends from start to finish'. Phillips gets closer: 'Jesus, the source and the goal of our faith'. Perhaps best of all is the Revised Standard Version: 'Jesus the pioneer and perfecter of our faith'. We look at the word 'pioneer' today, 'perfecter' tomorrow.

The word 'pioneer' is not often used of Jesus in the New Testament. The Acts of the Apostles uses it to describe Jesus as the one 'who has led the way to life' (3.15) and again as 'leader' (5.31). It can be used of a man who, when a ship is wrecked some distance from the shore, being a strong swimmer, ties a rope around him and heads out to land, thus making it possible for others to follow him from peril to safety. This, says our writer, is what our Lord has done. Crucified, risen, ascended, understanding, ever-present, he has led the way. We follow.

'*We* follow'–yes. But we are only a tiny part of those who down the ages have followed. We are surrounded with a great cloud of witnesses. We are not alone. We may be in a minority, but there are 'serried ranks of witnesses' (J. B. Phillips) gone on before. 'Think', then, 'of him', the pioneer, and think too of them. We believe in the communion of saints!

Almighty God, you have knit together your elect into one communion and fellowship in the mystical body of your Son. Give us grace so to follow your blessed saints in all virtuous and godly living, that we may come to those unspeakable joys which you have prepared for those who truly love you; through Jesus Christ our Lord.

HOLY WEEK Wednesday

READING Hebrews 12.1–10

And what of ourselves? With all these witnesses to faith around us like a cloud, we
must throw off every encumbrance, every sin to which we cling, and run with
resolution the race for which we are entered, 2our eyes fixed on Jesus, on whom
faith depends from start to finish: Jesus who, for the sake of the joy that lay ahead of
him, endured the cross, making light of its disgrace, and has taken his seat at the
right hand of the throne of God.
3Think of him who submitted to such opposition from sinners: that will help you
not to lose heart and grow faint. 4In your struggle against sin, you have not yet
resisted to the point of shedding your blood. 5You have forgotten the text of
Scripture which addresses you as sons and appeals to you in these words:

'My son, do not think lightly of the Lord's discipline,
nor lose heart when he corrects you;
6for the Lord disciplines those whom he loves;
he lays the rod on every son whom he acknowledges.'

7You must endure it as discipline: God is treating you as sons. Can anyone be a son,
who is not disciplined by his father? 8If you escape the discipline in which all sons
share, you must be bastards and no true sons. 9Again, we paid due respect to the
earthly fathers who disciplined us; should we not submit even more readily to our
spiritual Father, and so attain life? 10They disciplined us for this short life according
to their lights; but he does so for our true welfare, so that we may share his holiness.

PERFECTER

This is the only occurrence in the New Testament of this word as a title of Jesus–finisher, perfecter, goal (v.2). He is the one towards whom we move, the one whom we always keep in our mind's eye–his will, our will. On him our 'faith depends from start to finish'.

'Perfecter' suggests that he will not abandon what he has started. He has begun to 'bring many sons to glory' (2.10). He has set his hand to this plough and he will never look back till the work is finished. He will see it through. We can thank God for that.

The process may–indeed will–entail suffering for the disciple. But if this is regarded as the discipline of a loving Father, like a refining process for purifying silver, we shall see that our true welfare is in view, nothing less than sharing God's holiness (v.10).

Our elder brother, Jesus himself, has trodden that road ahead of us. He endured what we never shall, the cross, and made light of its disgrace. That was his road to glory. He did it knowing 'the joy that lay ahead of him', or (for the original can be translated in both ways) he endured the cross 'in place of the joy that was open to him'.

'Think of him', the perfecter, and go on thinking of him in the closing days of this Holy Week!

Almighty God, whose most dear Son went not up to joy but first he suffered pain, and entered not into glory before he was crucified: mercifully grant that we, walking in the way of the cross, may find it none other than the way of life and peace; through Jesus Christ our Lord.

MAUNDY THURSDAY

READING Hebrews 9.11–15

But now Christ has come, high priest of good things already in being. The tent of his
priesthood is a greater and more perfect one, not made by men's hands, that is, not
belonging to this created world; [12]the blood of his sacrifice is his own blood, not the
blood of goats and calves; and thus he has entered the sanctuary once and for all and
secured an eternal deliverance. [13]For if the blood of goats and bulls and the
sprinkled ashes of a heifer have power to hallow those who have been defiled and
restore their external purity, [14]how much greater is the power of the blood of Christ;
he offered himself without blemish to God, a spiritual and eternal sacrifice; and his
blood will cleanse our conscience from the deadness of our former ways and fit us
for the service of the living God.
[15]And therefore he is the mediator of a new covenant, or testament, under which,
now that there has been a death to bring deliverance from sins committed under the
former covenant, those whom God has called may receive the promise of the
eternal inheritance.

MEDIATOR

Two concepts, basic to the biblical writers, meet in v.15–those of *covenant* and of *mediator*.

In the Bible God is often represented as taking the initiative in getting into touch with men, making an agreement or *covenant* with them on certain conditions (for example, with Noah, with Abraham, with Moses). Such covenant-making is an indication of God's loving concern for his people and of his desire for a right and happy relationship with them. The Old Testament is in large part taken up with the sad story of man's rejection or breaking of God's covenants.

A *mediator* is thought of as one who intervenes between two parties who need to be drawn together or reconciled. The writer of the Epistle to the Hebrews makes much of this idea and concentrates it all on Christ. He is God's representative to man and also, as perfect man, is man's representative to God. As Son of God, he is able to represent God perfectly and also, since he shares with us our flesh and blood, he is able to be a merciful and faithful mediator and high priest.

Man has been alienated from God by his sin and guilt. Man in his sin needs more than a prophet to reveal to him what is the mind and will of God. He needs a mediator who will reconcile him to God. The glory of the gospel is that both revelation and reconciliation are provided for him in Christ. Of this Christ has given us assurance in the institution of the new covenant in his blood, of which we think with deep thankfulness this Maundy Thursday.

Grant us so to reverence the sacred mysteries of your body and blood,
that we may know within ourselves and show forth in our lives
the fruits of your redemption.

GOOD FRIDAY

READING Hebrews 4. 14–16; 7. 23–28

Since therefore we have a great high priest who has passed through the heavens, Jesus the Son of God, let us hold fast to the religion we profess. 15For ours is not a high priest unable to sympathize with our weaknesses, but one who, because of his likeness to us, has been tested every way, only without sin. 16Let us therefore boldly approach the throne of our gracious God, where we may receive mercy and in his grace find timely help.

23Those other priests are appointed in numerous succession, because they are prevented by death from continuing in office; 24but the priesthood which Jesus holds is perpetual, because he remains for ever. 25That is why he is also able to save absolutely those who approach God through him; he is always living to plead on their behalf.

26Such a high priest does indeed fit our condition–devout, guileless, undefiled, separated from sinners, raised high above the heavens. 27He has no need to offer sacrifices daily, as the high priests do, first for his own sins and then for those of the people; for this he did once and for all when he offered up himself. 28The high priests made by the Law are men in all their frailty; but the priest appointed by the words of the oath which supersedes the Law is the Son, made perfect now for ever.

HIGH PRIEST

We noticed in passing when we were studying 3.1–6 (Apostle), that Jesus was spoken of as High Priest. This is one of the favourite concepts of the writer of the Epistle to the Hebrews–a large part of his book is given to the consideration of this aspect of Christ's person and work.

The idea of a sacrificial system in which priests offered up animal sacrifices as a regular religious routine is foreign to modern western thought. Nevertheless, it is worth while taking considerable care to understand the main ideas which lay behind the system–the holiness of God, the sinfulness of man, the utter necessity of a right relationship between man and God, and so on. These things are of abiding and universal importance.

This epistle sets out a series of contrasts between the work and achievements of the High Priests of the old dispensation and those of Christ, our great High Priest. Their work had to be repeated constantly; his was once for all. Their work could not effectively atone for deliberate sin; Christ's could and did. High priests were many in number, a succession of them carrying on the work; Christ was without peer, risen, ascended, and deathless. They offered animal sacrifices; he offered himself in total unblemished obedience.

As today we ponder on the meaning of the Cross, let us thank God for Jesus, our great High Priest, 'tested every way' even to death, 'able to sympathize with our weaknesses' (4.15), 'able to save absolutely those who approach God through him' (7.25).

Though now ascended up on high,
He bends on earth a brother's eye;
Partaker of the human name,
He knows the frailty of our frame.

In every pang that rends the heart
The Man of Sorrows had a part;
He sympathizes with our grief,
And to the sufferer sends relief.

EASTER EVE

READING 1 Corinthians 5.7–8

> The old leaven of corruption is working among you. Purge it out, and then you will be bread of a new baking. As Christians you are unleavened Passover bread; for indeed our Passover has begun; the sacrifice is offered–Christ himself. [8]So we who observe the festival must not use the old leaven, the leaven of corruption and wickedness, but only the unleavened bread which is sincerity and truth.

OUR PASSOVER

In many parts of the Christian world tonight, the Great Vigil of Easter will be celebrated. The minds of millions will turn to Christ, to think of him as the true Paschal Lamb. That is to say, they will recall the story of Exodus 12, in which the children of Israel were told to celebrate annually their deliverance from Egypt, and to do it by an animal sacrifice. All leaven was to be cleaned out from their houses; only unleavened bread was to be eaten.

St Paul in these verses sees a 'fulfilment' of this old story in Christ. He, God's provision for man's sin and need, has been sacrificed for us. A foe greater than Egypt, sin and death itself, has been defeated. Christians, entering into that victory, must separate themselves from all 'corruption and wickedness', as the Israelites swept out all traces of yeast, and be marked only by 'sincerity and truth'.

As Christ died and was buried in the tomb, so are we to die to sin and rise with him to a new life of holiness and service. In thankfulness, and in preparation for Easter Day, let us, in the presence of God, engage in an act of recollection:

> This is the night when you brought our fathers, the children of Israel, out of bondage in Egypt, and led them through the Red Sea on dry land.
>
> This is the night when all who believe in Christ are delivered from the gloom of sin, and are restored to grace and holiness of life.
>
> This is the night when Christ broke the bonds of death and hell, and rose victorious from the grave.
>
> How wonderful and beyond our knowing, O God, is your mercy and loving-kindness to us, that to redeem a slave you gave a Son.
>
> How blessed is this night when earth and heaven are joined and man is reconciled to God.

EASTER DAY

READING Revelation 1.10–18

It was on the Lord's day, and I was caught up by the Spirit; and behind me I heard a
loud voice, like the sound of a trumpet, [11]which said to me, 'Write down what you
see on a scroll and send it to the seven churches: to Ephesus, Smyrna, Pergamum,
Thyatira, Sardis, Philadelphia, and Laodicea.' I turned to see whose voice it was
that spoke to me; and when I turned I saw seven standing lamps of gold, [13]and
among the lamps one like a son of man, robed down to his feet, with a golden girdle
round his breast. [14]The hair of his head was white as snow-white wool, and his eyes
flamed like fire; [15]his feet gleamed like burnished brass refined in a furnace, and his
voice was like the sound of rushing waters. [16]In his right hand he held seven stars,
and out of his mouth came a sharp two-edged sword; and his face shone like the sun
in full strength.

[17]When I saw him, I fell at his feet as though dead. But he laid his right hand upon
me and said, 'Do not be afraid. I am the first and the last, [18]and I am the living one;
for I was dead and now I am alive for evermore, and I hold the keys of Death and
Death's domain.'

RESURRECTION

It is more than possible that when you go to church this morning you will hear this passage read from the Book of the Revelation. Picture the scene: a man deported because he had preached God's word and borne his testimony to Jesus (v.9)–deported to a little island, probably to slave away in the mines. Cut off from fellowship with other Christians and deprived of his eucharistic worship, he recalls that it is 'the Lord's day' (v.10), the day of resurrection, and his spirit lifts. He hears a voice; he receives a vision. It is a vision of the risen Christ–the first and the last . . . the living one, who was dead and now is alive for evermore . . . who holds the keys of Death and Death's domain. How can he be depressed any longer? Christ is risen! *Christus Victor*!

The claim of Jesus to be 'the resurrection' (John 11.25) has been made good. The forces of sin and death have been overcome.

I shall not forget the first time that I saw in a friend's study a wooden statue of Christ reigning from the Cross. Here was no drooping figure of agony. Here was one robed in majesty, head erect. Crucifixion and resurrection power were combined; Good Friday and Easter Day were represented as one mighty act. The Lamb who had been slain was the one who held the keys.

He still is. Hallelujah!

Hail the Lord of earth and heaven!
Praise to thee by both be given;
Thee we greet triumphant now;
Hail, the Resurrection thou!

O come, let us adore him.